The Life and Work of...

Auguste Rodin

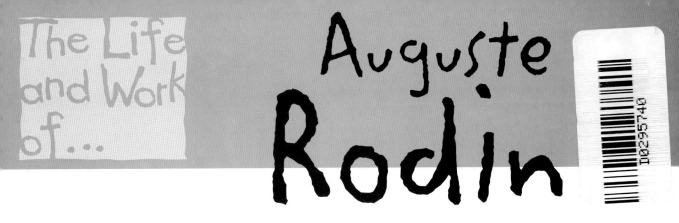

Richard Tames

Heinemann
LIBRARY

H www.heinemann.co.uk
Visit our website to find out more information about Heinemann Library books.

To order:
☎ Phone 44 (0) 1865 888066
▤ Send a fax to 44 (0) 1865 314091
🖥 Visit the Heinemann Bookshop at www.heinemann.co.uk to browse our catalogue and order online.

First published in Great Britain by Heinemann Library, Halley Court, Jordan Hill, Oxford OX2 8EJ a division of Reed Educational and Professional Publishing Ltd.
Heinemann is a registered trademark of Reed Educational & Professional Publishing Ltd.

OXFORD MELBOURNE AUCKLAND
JOHANNESBURG BLANTYRE GABORONE
IBADAN PORTSMOUTH (NH) USA CHICAGO

Designed by Celia Floyd
Originated by Dot Gradations
Printed in Hong Kong/China

04 03 02 01 00
10 9 8 7 6 5 4 3 2 1

ISBN 0 431 091986

British Library Cataloguing in Publication Data

Tames, Richard, 1946–
  Life and work of Auguste Rodin
  1. Rodin, Auguste, 1840-1917 – Juvenile literature
  2. Sculptors – France – Biography – Juvenile literature
  3. Sculpture, Modern, 19th century – France – Juvenile literature
  4. Painting, French – Juvenile literature
  I. Title   II. Auguste Rodin
  730.9'2

Acknowledgements
The Publishers would like to thank the following for permission to reproduce photographs:

Bridgeman Art Library: Musee d'Orsay, Paris p21; Musée Rodin, Paris: pp4, 6, 14, 20, Hélène Moulonguet p7, Adam Rzepka pp5, 9, 13, 18, 25, Charles Aubry pp10,12, Erik and Petra Hesmerg p11, Bruno Jarret p15, Jessie Lipscomb p16, Jêrome Manoukian pp17, 23, Pierre Bonnard p22, Edward Steichen 24, Choumoff p28, Jean de Calan p29; Photo RMN: R G Ojeda p19; Roger-Viollet: Harlingue-Viollet p26; Trip: Christopher Rennie p27

Cover photograph reproduced with permission of AKG London

Every effort has been made to contact copyright holders of any material reproduced in this book. Any omissions will be rectified in subsequent printings if notice is given to the Publisher.

Any words appearing in the text in bold, **like this**, are explained in the Glossary.

Contents

Who was Auguste Rodin?

Auguste Rodin was a French artist and **sculptor**. He is most famous for the **statues** of people he made out of clay, **bronze** and **marble**.

Auguste tried to show feelings in his **sculptures**. The people in this sculpture are unhappy because their city in France has been taken over by an English king.

Early years

Auguste was born in Paris, France on 12 November 1840. This is a photograph of Auguste aged 9 and his mother. He started drawing when he was 10 years old.

Auguste went to a special drawing school when he was 14. He began to make clay models at 15. His **sculptures** were based on his drawings of people.

Hard times

Auguste began to earn money making stone decorations for buildings. When his sister died in 1862 he was very sad and he tried to become a **monk**. But he soon returned to his work.

When Auguste had to work for other people in the day, he worked on his own models in the evenings. He was only 19 when he made this head of his father.

Great changes

In 1864, when he was 24, Auguste met Rose Beuret. She **posed** for him and was his helper for the rest of his life. Auguste got his first **studio**. It was a cold, damp stable.

Auguste and Rose had a son, called Auguste, in 1866. Auguste made this **bust** of a young woman the year after he met Rose. It is called *Young Woman in a Flowered Hat.*

Leaving Paris

To earn enough money to feed his family, Auguste left Paris to work in Belgium from 1871 to 1875. In 1875 he went to Italy for a year where he studied the work of the **sculptor** Michelangelo.

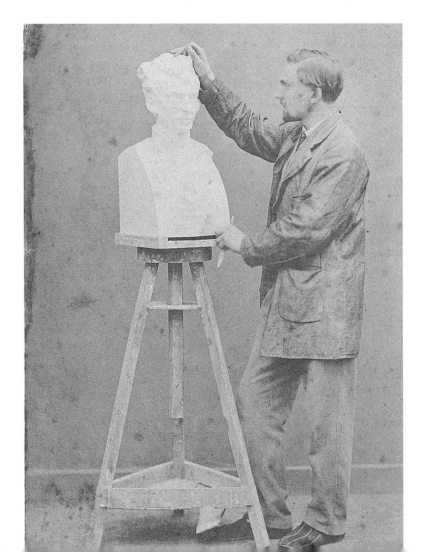

Auguste wanted to become famous. But his *Man with the Broken Nose* was turned down for an important **exhibition**. Many people did not like Auguste's realistic style.

Fame at last

Auguste had to wait until he was almost 40 to become famous. But his life-size **statue** of a soldier, which he called *Age of Bronze*, brought him problems, too.

The *Age of Bronze* looked so real that some people said Auguste cheated. After this, he made his statues bigger or smaller than life-size, to prove he did not cheat.

The work of a lifetime

In 1880, Auguste was asked to make a huge doorway for a museum in Paris. He based his drawings for it on the way the Italian poet Dante described Hell. It was called *The Gates of Hell*.

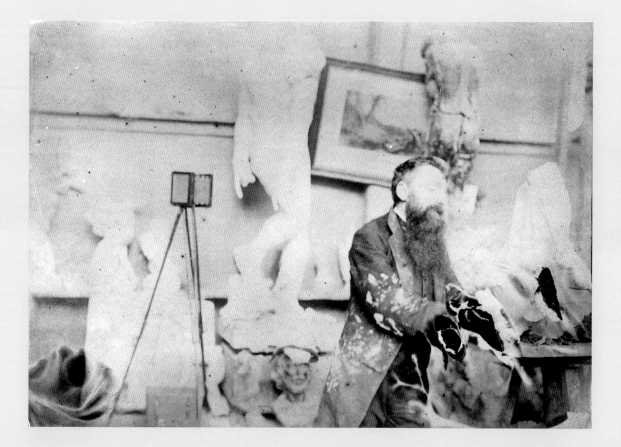

Auguste's most famous **statue**, *The Thinker*, is meant to be Dante. It was meant to go on the top of the *Gates of Hell*.

Camille

This **bust** of Auguste was made by the **sculptor** Camille Claudel in 1888. Auguste liked the bust very much. Camille helped Rodin with his work. She also **posed** for him.

Camille posed for this **sculpture**. It is called *Thought* and Auguste made it in 1888. In it Camille is wearing a hat usually worn by brides in northern France.

A big studio

Auguste moved to Meudon, near Paris. Here he had a big new **studio** with lots of space. He often had up to 50 helpers there. They made **carvings** from his clay models.

Rodin loved to read, and he got a lot of ideas from books. In 1897 he made this **bust** of the great French writer Victor Hugo, who wrote the *Hunchback of Notre Dame.*

Famous faces

Auguste liked making **busts** of his friends or people he wanted to thank. This picture shows him making a bust of the French **sculptor** Jean Alexandre Falguière.

Auguste showed this **statue** of the French writer Honoré de Balzac in 1898. Auguste read Balzac's books so he could understand him better.

Success

In 1900 Auguste had his first big **exhibition** in Paris. It included over 150 of his **sculptures**. People came from all over the world to see his work.

Auguste called this sculpture the *Cathedral*. He thought that the two hands raised together looked like the pointed arches in cathedrals.

Home and museum

In 1903 Auguste had a **biography** written about him. It was written by the German poet Rainer Maria Rilke. This picture shows Rainer with Rose and Auguste and their dogs outside their house at Meudon.

Rainer invited Auguste to the Hotel Biron in Paris. This building became Auguste's home. Today it is the Rodin Museum, where people come to see examples of his best work.

Last days

Auguste married Rose on 29 January 1917. She died two weeks later on 14 February 1917. He died on 17 November 1917. They were buried together at Meudon under a copy of Auguste's **statue** of *The Thinker*.

When Rodin died, one of his greatest works, *The Gates of Hell*, was left unfinished. It can be seen at the Rodin Museum in Paris.

Timeline

1840   Rene-Francois-Auguste Rodin born on 12 November.

1853   The artist Vincent van Gogh is born in Holland.

1854   Auguste goes to drawing school.

1857   Auguste fails to get into art college.

1862–1863 Auguste tries to become a **monk**.

1864   Auguste meets Rose Beuret.

1870   Auguste joins the army.

1871   Auguste leaves the army and moves to Belgium.

1875–1876 Auguste travels in Italy to study art.

1877   Auguste moves back to Paris.

1879   The artist Paul Klee is born.

1880   Auguste is asked to make *The Gates of Hell*.

1897   Auguste moves to Meudon.

1898   The **sculptor** Henry Moore is born.

1900   Auguste shows 150 sculptures at a Paris exhibition.

1903   Rainer Maria Rilke writes Auguste's biography.

1908   King Edward VII of England visits Auguste's studio.

1914   Auguste publishes a book on the **cathedrals** of France.

1914–1918 World War I.

1917   Auguste dies on 17 November.

Glossary

biography story of a person's life

bronze metal made of tin and copper

bust statue of a head and shoulders

carvings object carved (cut out) of wood or rock

cathedral main church of a big city

exhibition show of art in public

John the Baptist preacher who lived at the same time as Jesus (He performed baptisms – the ceremony by which people become members of the Christian church.)

marble special kind of limestone rock

monk man who devotes his whole life to his religion

pose stand or sit in a certain way while someone paints or draws you

sculptor person who makes statues or carvings

sculpture statue or carving

statue carved, moulded or sculpted figure of a person or animal

studio special room or building where an artist works

More books to read

Henry Moore, Sean Connolly, Heinemann Library

Michelangelo Buonarroti, Richard Tames, Heinemann Library

More art to see

The Kiss, Tate Gallery, London

Copies of Auguste Rodin's work can also be seen in: Victoria and Albert Museum, London; The Burrell Collection, Glasgow; National Museum of Wales, Cardiff; Museum and Art Gallery, Walsall, West Midlands; Aberdeen Art Gallery.

Index